SPECIAL EVENTS
IN THE CHURCH

PROGRAM BUILDER No. 2

Compiled by Paul M. Miller

Contents

Lillenas Publishing Co.
KANSAS CITY, MO. 64141

Celebrating the Church

A Program for a Groundbreaking Ceremony

By Esther M. Bailey

Pastor—The purpose of our gathering today is to get started on the program that we believe God has called us to undertake. We vision a new church building (or addition) as a place where believers can worship God, a place where those who don't know Jesus can find Him, a place that will be inviting to children, a place of fellowship for the lonely. This building will be different things to different people, but the overall goal of the church is to meet the needs of individuals whatever they might be.

As I turn over this first shovel of dirt, I want it to represent my burden for the community as a whole. I'm concerned because lives are being destroyed by sin and I trust that our work here will result in changed lives in people whose sins are buried far deeper than this shovel can penetrate.

Now, as I pass the shovel to various members of our congregation representing specific interests, may we form a circle linked together by holding hands as indication of our unity in undertaking this work.

Board of Trustee Member—For the board of trustees, digging into this soil represents the business aspect of our commitment. Money will need to be raised, quotes must be procured and compared, contracts will need to be negotiated and signed. There will be personal sacrifices required of each of us, but the result will be a better place in which to conduct God's business.

Nursery Director—As director of the Nursery Department, I turn over a shovel of dirt to represent the new lives that will be coming into our congregation. We hope there will be many children who will grow up in this church, whose lives will be formed by Christian principles and eventually transformed by the power of the Holy Spirit.

Board of Christian Education Member—On behalf of the entire educational aspect of the church, I dig into a section of new ground to represent a new start in Christian education. Our teaching facilities will be expanded through the completion of this work. Our long-term goals include a dedication to working out attractive programs, a concerted effort to reach the unchurched through Bible school or

2

Sunday School rallies, and manifestation of a spirit of love and friendliness that will bring new contacts to the church.

Sunday School Superintendent—I break up a portion of the soil as if preparing it for cultivation, because, in effect, that is what we are doing. Each Sunday morning teachers will stand before small groups of learners, separated according to age or interests. These will be dedicated teachers planting the Word of God as seeds to take root and grow. Let us pray that much of the seed will fall on good ground.

Youth Director—I need to take extra care in lifting this shovel of dirt from the ground because it represents the urgent needs of our young people. During the critical teen years it's easy to drift away from the church—away from God. We need to prepare ourselves to understand the developmental process as the child moves toward adulthood. By combining knowledge with the love of God, we can minimize the relentless efforts of Satan to snatch our young people from the fold.

Family Life Counselor—The structure of this ground can readily be altered. With a thrust of the shovel I can lift up a section of loose soil, then reshape it as I wish. So it is that the church can mold the family life of the community by offering Christian guidelines for interaction between husband and wife, parents and children. There is no greater opportunity for evangelism than through services to the family.

Music Committee Member—I wish I knew how to add a musical quality to the sound of this dirt as it is being scooped up, because I vision this church as a great witness to God through music. As evidence of our intent to preach the Word of God through song, let us join together in singing _____.

Coordinator of Golden Agers—Sometimes the elder saints become forgotten sheep, but may it not happen here. I'd like to think of this shovel of upturned soil as representative of our geriatric ministry. It's important to provide spiritual and emotional stimulation to our older church members so that they may continue to be growing persons.

Missionary Committee Member—Instead of lifting a shovel of soil from the general area of excavation, I'd like to move to untouched territory. This is our way of taking the gospel to the uttermost parts of the earth. We realize that the spiritual life of the church is directly linked to our willingness to carry out the Great Commission.

Pastor—As we launch into this building program, may these objectives govern every act we perform—every decision we make.

(Closes the service with prayer.)

Dedication Service

By Irene B. Brand

Leader—One thing have I desired of the Lord, that will I seek after; that I may dwell in the house of the Lord all the days of my life, to behold the beauty of the Lord, and to inquire in his temple (Psalm 27:4).

Congregation—We are grateful for the great builders of the past who left us a rich heritage in church buildings.

Leader—How amiable are thy tabernacles, O Lord of hosts! (Psalm 84:1).

Congregation—We dedicate this building in memory of all those who have gone before, who have served this church with loyal hearts and hands.

Leader—My soul longeth, yea, even fainteth for the courts of the Lord: my heart and my flesh crieth out for the living God (Psalm 84:2).

Congregation—We dedicate this building in gratitude for those of our present fellowship who have made this renovation (construction) possible.

Leader—Blessed is the man whose strength is in thee; in whose heart are the ways of them (Psalm 84:5).

Congregation—We dedicate this sanctuary to the worship and service of Almighty God.

Leader—For a day in thy courts is better than a thousand. I had rather be a door-keeper in the house of my God, than to dwell in the tents of wickedness (Psalm 84:10).

Congregation—We dedicate this building to the training of children in the knowledge of the Bible, and to the calling of youth into full-time Christian service.

Leader—I was glad when they said unto me, Let us go into the house of the Lord (Psalm 122:1).

Congregation—We dedicate this building to the saving of souls, the comfort of the discouraged, and the strengthening of the faithful.

Leader—But will God indeed dwell on the earth? behold, the heaven and heaven of heavens cannot contain thee; how much less this house that I have builded? (1 Kings 8:27).

Congregation—We dedicate this house to the worldwide Christian missionary endeavor.

Leader—Enter into his gates with thanksgiving, and into his courts with praise: be thankful unto him, and bless his name (Psalm 100:4).

Congregation—Praise God, from whom all blessings flow!

Capsule Commission

Devotional thoughts for a church dedication

By Ethel V. Leffel

(Prior to the occasion, prepare copies of the dedication pledge which follows leader's remarks.)

LEADER—Our purpose in gathering here today is to dedicate our new church building to God, and to rededicate ourselves to the carrying out of the commission that Jesus gave to His followers to win the world to himself. We are going to turn to God's Word for inspiration so that we may know His will and have the certain knowledge that if we use His Word as a guide in our new venture, He will bless both us and the work of His church.

Our text is found in John 20:19-22. In these few verses, we have a capsule commission. We have the complete formula for the success of our commitment. The five key words are: Presence, Peace, Person, Purpose, Power.

Presence:

The 19th verse of our text "Jesus [came] and stood in the midst [of them]." After the Crucifixion the close followers of Jesus sensed fear and defeat. They were assembled in secret for fear of the Jews. While they were in this state of mind Jesus came and stood in their midst. His very presence must have calmed them.

Is there a sense of fear in your hearts in these troubled times? We are living in fearful days. The Bible tells us that things will get worse and worse before Jesus comes again. The work of the Church will encounter more opposition as the days pass. Is there a remedy for us? Yes, there is! We need only to go to the Word. There we find that the presence of Jesus in our midst is a reality. If we really believe this, we will be ready for the task that is ours as the Body of Christ, His Church.

Peace:

The next word that we want to notice is the word *peace*. Speaking to those fearful disciples, Jesus greeted them. "Peace be unto you," He said.

How the disciples must have longed for peace! How the world has always longed for peace! But we know that there can be no real peace outside of a genuine faith in God, and in knowing what His Word says. But isn't Jesus called the Prince of Peace? Didn't the angels proclaim peace to the world at His birth? Where is the peace?

The peace had to be in their hearts. Peace in the world wasn't what He granted to them. Now they must understand that there was a task to do before real peace could be realized, and to accomplish this task, they must obey Him implicitly. The warfare they had to face was not a worldly warfare. It was a warfare with spiritual principalities and powers. It was to be a battle between God and the evil powers for the souls of men. They needed to know that even in the worst of trials, there is true peace in Him.

Do we have the peace of Jesus to use as a weapon in the task before us? Are we at peace with God so that we can give peace to others? Jesus said, "Peace be unto you." This is for us as well as for those fearful disciples.

Person:

Our text goes on to say, "He shewed unto them his hands and his side. Then were the disciples glad, when they saw the Lord." He had to show them His person so that they would believe that He was the Christ who had hung on the Cross just three days prior to this. Thomas wasn't the only one who needed to see this. The other disciples needed it, too, and so do we.

Unless we realize that the Jesus we worship is the Jesus of Calvary, the Lamb of God who died for the sin of the world and for your sins and mine, we are worshipping in vain, and our dedication is in vain. Jesus will carry the nail-scarred hands and the wounded side into eternity. He is indeed the Son of God. This belief is essential to the success of our dedication today.

Purpose:

In verse 21 Jesus states the task that was His and which He is passing on to them. He says, "As my Father hath sent me, even so send I you." What could be clearer? This is still the purpose of the Church of Jesus Christ today. It is your purpose for being, and it is mine.

Let us today rededicate ourselves and our church to be co-workers with Him in witnessing to the world not only in our small area, but to the uttermost corners of the earth!

Power:

Our last word is not least in importance. It is the most essential ingredient for success in our consecration to God. Jesus breathed on them and said, "Receive ye the Holy Ghost."

Was that power only for them? No! In John 14 Jesus made a startling statement. *(Leader reads verse 12.)*

In Jesus' name, we, His Church, have dwelling in our very hearts the Holy Spirit of Almighty God. We have, in Jesus' name, tremendous power at our disposal. Moreover, we have the blood of Christ, His resurrection power, and His authority at the very throne of God.

"All power is given unto me," He says. Then He adds, "Go ye!" What is this power for? It is given to us so that we can accomplish the tremendous task that is ours!

Let us in Jesus' name tap into this great resource as we dedicate ourselves to God today!

(Leader prepares congregation to repeat pledge.)

Let us together dedicate this building and rededicate ourselves as we in faith look to God for guidance. Please repeat with me:

We dedicate this building and we rededicate ourselves to the work that Jesus left for us to do.

We believe in His *presence*. His Word says, "Where two or three are gathered together in my name, there am I in the midst of them."

We covet His perfect *peace*. God's Word says, "I will keep him in perfect peace, whose mind is stayed on Thee."

We recognize His *person:* God's Word says, "This same Jesus, who was taken up into heaven, shall so come in like manner as ye have seen him go."

We realize our *purpose:* His Word says, "Go ye into all the world, and preach the gospel to every creature."

We open our hearts to His *power:* His Word says, "Ye shall receive power, after that the Holy Spirit has come upon you: and you shall be witnesses unto me in Jerusalem, Judaea, and in all Samaria, and unto the uttermost part of the earth."

As a congregation, we pledge ourselves to serve Christ in the power of the Holy Spirit and a spirit of unity with Christ and with each other, and in so doing to fulfill the purpose of this new edifice that God has enabled us to build.

Dedicatory prayer.

Installation of Pastor

HYMN: "Saviour, like a Shepherd Lead Us"

SCRIPTURE: 1 Timothy 6:10-21

FORMAL INTRODUCTION OF PASTOR TO CONGREGATION

(Response of congregation from printed copies.)

LEADER—Having called this man as your pastor, do you solemnly swear to pray for him and work with him?

CONGREGATION—We do.

LEADER—Do you promise to listen and participate in each sermon?

CONGREGATION—We do.

LEADER—Do you consecrate your gifts?

CONGREGATION—We do.

LEADER—Do you consecrate your service?

CONGREGATION—We do.

LEADER—Do you consecrate your talents and monies?

CONGREGATION—We do.

LEADER *(turning to pastor)*—Do you promise to be a good shepherd to this people, to love and cherish them?

PASTOR—I do.

LEADER—Do you vow to minister to the needs of all alike?

PASTOR—I do.

LEADER—Do you promise to be a friend to all who are willing?

PASTOR—I do.

LEADER—Do you promise to preach God's Word in season and out of season?

PASTOR—I do.

LEADER—Do you vow to seek the salvation of the lost and nurture the saved?

PASTOR—I do.

LEADER—Then may God bless you and this congregation in this ministry!

PRAYER BY LEADER AND PASTOR

—Gean D. Smith

For a Church Anniversary

God hitherto has brought us,
   His Church, His cherished Bride.
Here precious things He's taught us;
   Our needs have been supplied.

Still farther shall He lead us,
   To heights yet unattained,
And shepherds send to feed us,
   Whom He for us ordained.

Through gifts and intercession
   We'll spread the gospel wide,
Till not a single nation
   Shall be God's Word denied.

Till every tribe blends voices
   In grateful song above;
And the whole church rejoices
   In oneness and in love.

—Anna Marie Dahlquist

We Dedicate This Organ

We dedicate this organ,
   Our Father, God, to Thee,
Creator of skill and of music,
   Of rhythm and melody.

We dedicate this organ,
   O Jesus Christ, to Thee,
Who can change our clashing anguish
   Into peace and harmony.

We dedicate this organ,
   O Holy Spirit, to Thee;
Use it to speak to our spirits
   About what God wants us to be.

We dedicate this organ
   To the Blessed Trinity;
Oh, use it for Thy glory;
   Lift our hearts in praise to Thee!

—Anna Marie Dahlquist

For the Dedication of a Memorial Building

We dedicate this building now,
   O Architect of Majesty,
In memory of Thy servant true°
   Who built a spiritual house for
      Thee.

In memory of that poured-out life,
   Each brick which we see here was
      laid,
With hopes this place should serve the
      work
   For which Thy servant daily prayed.

With stalwart faith Thy servant built
   A life where Christ was on the
      throne,
And on the True Foundation placed
   Gold, silver, and many a precious
      stone.

So now we dedicate this place,
   Remembering the past with praise,
And trusting for rich blessing here
   In all this building's future days.

—Anna Marie Dahlquist

°The name of a person may be substituted
for "Thy servant true."

Organ Dedication

This organ is dedicated to glorify
God through music. In years to come it
will bring forth from its keyboard,
songs to comfort the bereaved, marches
to thrill a bride's heart, accompaniment for solos, duets, trios, quartets,
the choir, and other instruments.

Its music will uplift during worship
and sadden during funerals. It will rejoice during revival, cause babies to
clap their hands, youth to tap their
feet, and many to praise their Lord.

This instrument is dedicated to the
Living God whose ears are always
tuned to the music of His people. May
it be used to richly bless the further-
ance of God's kingdom!

—Gean D. Smith

Housewarming

I saw a house all tumbling down and
  sad
  With rubbish piled, and patched up
  window-panes.
I saw it standing cold and gray and
  drab,
  Made grayer by the fog and
  drizzling rain.

No laughter rang throughout its empty
  halls;
  No lights to beckon on the
  windowsill.
No love that hung bright paper on the
  walls,
  Or sewed cool curtains with a lacy
  frill.

And then one day I walked in winter
  snow,
  And saw smoke curling skyward
  from the flue.
Saw children playing in the firelight
  glow,
  Through windowpanes all spanking
  clean and new.

And then I thought how love can turn
  the page,
  And eager willing hands make work
  well done.
For families make old houses come
  alive,
  And turn a lonely house into a
  home!

—*Ethel V. Leffel*

My Church

(To be recited by a child)

Thank You, dear God, for my church
  With walls so strong and carpet soft,
With stained-glass windows and
  balcony,
  With pulpit and choir loft.

Thank You, dear God, for the pastor
  Who makes Your Word so clear,
And thank You, dear Lord, for the
  choir;
  I listen, and know that You're near.

Thank You, dear God, for my church,
  It's for my parents and me,
And all my friends who come in
  To worship You lovingly.

—*Anna Marie Dahlquist*

A Mortgage-burning Ceremony

As guests gather for the mortgage-burning ceremony (for church or parsonage) give each a piece of an actual mortgage payment statement. Following selected stories and testimonies from people who were involved in the building's construction, prayer, and special music, allow each member of the congregation to drop his or her portion of the mortgage in a flaming metal container.

It may work well to have a giant reproduction of the mortgage document displayed in the front of the auditorium. Following the service, each member comes forward and tears a piece from the document and places it in the flame.

—*Martha Bolton*

Tribute and Appreciation

Comfort from a Comforter

by Jane K. Priewe

Choice of a farewell or retirement gift for your pastor or a missionary is always an important decision. A personal comforter is a lasting and cherished gift. It isn't too much work for one person, for many friends have a hand in its construction. But one person does have to organize the project. A personal comforter is made from many embroidered squares, all sewn together into a coverlet—an unforgettable and lovely gift.

First, decide who will make a square for the comforter. (They can be decorative, or simple squares with names embroidered on them.) Count on using more squares than you have names, for you are bound to forget someone or have newcomers to add at the last minute. Even if you don't get a taker for every square, plain colored blocks look pretty when mixed in with the embroidered ones. If you should wind up with too many embroidered squares you can turn them into scatter pillows for the bed, or a pillow bolster.

The beauty of the personal comforter is that the creator of each square can let her imagination take over. The different ideas will mean so much to the recipient of the comforter. Some ideas for blocks would be an embroidered family, including cat, dog, or whatever possession makes the family unique, such as old model car, a boat, or a swimming pool. If the family's last name is a common noun (Bush, Starr, Wheeler, Bell), embroider a bush, a star, a bell, or a wheel with an R.

Let the people know the size and type of material or provide squares in advance. The squares must be uniform in size, allowing for at least a half-inch seam on all sides. The more colorful your comforter is, the prettier it will be. The choice of materials is vast: permanent press, lightweight double knits, cotton, velvet. All blocks should be the same material. Allow plenty of time, but set a deadline, prodding dawdlers.

Once all squares are collected, lay them out in a color-coordinated, eye-pleasing pattern and sew them together in long rows before sewing the rows together in the finished product. To make seams meet, pin the blocks together before sewing.

Sew the backing in place, wrong sides together, leaving a short area on both sides of one corner to turn the comforter right side out. If desired, a flannel sheet or other filling may be used. Finish off by tying with bright, four-ply yarn.

Personal comforters can be made by youth groups, adult classes, women's groups, or a group of friends. Make the comforter presentation one of the highlights of your occasion.

Farewell to Pastor

By Esther M. Bailey

EMCEE—When there is a depth of feeling between two individuals, good-byes are always hard. That's what we're experiencing right now. That lump in your throat trying to hold back tears is a way of saying, "I don't want Pastor _____ to go."

Yes, this parting invokes a note of sadness as we think of what we're losing. But let's quench the inclination to downheartedness and concentrate on what we have gained from the _____ years that Pastor _____ has acted as our spiritual adviser. Several members of our congregation now wish to express special appreciation for the way in which Pastor _____'s ministry has touched their personal lives.

(The following paragraphs are guidelines representing common experiences in a typical congregation. Those who speak should select the one most appropriate, then tailor the speech to reflect their personal feelings. Some people may want to write an entirely new speech with emphasis on a personal theme not covered here.)

o   o   o

Sometimes the greatest service one individual can do for another is to introduce a third person. The newly formed association may result in a lifelong friendship, a business alliance or even a husband-wife relationship. It was that kind of permanent impact that Pastor _____'s ministry has had for me. His introduction of me to Jesus Christ turned my life around, healed my troubled soul, and named me among the heirs to God's eternal salvation.

o   o   o

Although I had accepted Jesus as Savior when I met Pastor _____, something was lacking from my Christian experience. The close fellowship with my Lord was missing; personal interests overshadowed commitment. Then Pastor _____'s sermons began to hit home. Through him, the Holy Spirit illumined my soul, turning my lukewarm testimony into determination to follow hard after the things of God.

o   o   o

I'm sure I must be a crisis-prone person. No one could get into the predicaments that I do without a built-in knack for trouble. Every time I call Pastor _____ it's something of an emergency: Help! Pray! What shall I do? He's been everything to me from (attending physician to investment adviser). When he goes, I'm going to have to relearn 1 Corinthians 10:13. I've come to read it like this: "God will not pile more trouble on you than you can handle and He will also provide a way of escape through Pastor _____."

11

I hate to think of what would have happened to me had Pastor _____-_____ not crossed my path at the right time. My family life was disintegrating; my children were about to add to the broken-home statistics. It was all set to happen, and nothing I could do would stop it. That was before Pastor _____-_____ showed me how the miraculous power of Jesus works. After I was healed from sin, it wasn't long before love started to repair the shattered foundation of our home.

o   o   o

Life-changing experiences is the general theme of this tribute we offer our pastor. I can attest to a life-changing experience in a very real sense. When I first knew Pastor _____, I was a child; now I am grown (*actual ages may be substituted*). The point that I would make emphasizes what didn't happen rather than what did. I'm thinking of the sorrow I have been *spared* because Pastor _____ influenced me at an early age to give my heart to Jesus.

o   o   o

Through my association with Pastor _____, I learned the joy that comes from taking an active role in the leadership phase of the church. When I believed I was too weak to serve, he encouraged me; when I realized my limitations due to lack of knowledge, he showed me how to receive instruction. If my work is acceptable before God, much of the credit belongs to Pastor _____-_____ for his support of me as I struggled to find my place in God's kingdom.

o   o   o

A service honoring our pastor would not be complete without a special tribute to his wife. Not only has she stood behind Pastor _____, sharing his burdens, supporting him with her prayers, but she herself has assumed responsibility for many aspects of his ministry. (*These should be enumerated.*) On behalf of the entire congregation, I focus the spotlight on Sister _____-_____ as we offer an expression of appreciation for her contribution to our spiritual well-being.

o   o   o

As I listen to these statements of gratitude for the work of Pastor _____ and his wife, I can't help but feel that I, too, have a small part in their accomplishments. You see, I was on the pulpit committee when the _____ were called to minister to this church. I'd like to say that I knew all along how great they would be, but I have to admit that their achievements have exceeded even my expectations.

EMCEE—The reason we love Pastor _____ and his wife so much is that God works through them. I'm sure they would remind us that, although *they* are leaving us, *God* isn't. We'll miss the _____ but we still have the Source of every good thing. We thank Pastor _____ and his wife for their labor of love with us and we wish them well as they continue their ministry elsewhere.

(*The pastor may wish to say a few words of farewell here. Prayer should follow, either led by the pastor or the emcee.*)

Tribute to a Christian Worker

(Golden or silver anniversary of Christian service, or for a retirement tribute.)

Your treasure chest is filled today,
    Not with stubble, hay, or wood,
But silver, gold, and precious stones
    Which the test of time have stood.

You've gathered wealth where no one
        steals;
    It's safe from moth and mold;
And the record of your selfless toils
    Won't yellow or grow old.

You've beat out something that will
        stand,
    You've carved what will endure;
Your silver and gold in a world of sand
    Is treasure that is sure.

—*Anna Marie Dahlquist*

Retirement Farewell

When you came here you walked real
        fast;
    Now you walk real slow.
You've been here for *(blank)* years;
    (Don't you think it's time to go?)

Just because we're so nice to you
    Doesn't mean you have to stay.
For *(blank)* long years you've stayed
        around here;
    (Why don't you just go away!)

Go away on a hunting trip;
    Or a vacation down by the sea.
Or find the thrill, of climbing a hill
    (Never plagued by the likes of me!)

You've been here for most of your life;
    And we just want you to know.
No other face will take your place;
    We will miss you whenever you go!

—*Gean D. Smith*

A Salute to the Custodian

The keeper of the church, you see
    Though called of God, should
        sturdy be.
For there are sundry tasks to do
    To keep a building looking new.

To close each window—lock each
        door;
    Check the lights, exits, fans, and
        more;
And pick up after children's "glee"—
    All these challenge his memory.

He, too, must have a watchful eye.
    A ring was lost, so he must try
To find the jewel—and Bible, too
    And things like buckles from a shoe.

The church custodian must be
    Patient and working cheerfully;
Faithfully moving chairs and screens
    And countless things behind the
        scenes.

God's blessings on this faithful one
    Whose jobs may seem like never
        done!
We're glad you answered God's good
        call—
    We salute the keeper of it all.

—*Carolyn Lehman*

13

Musings of a Sunday School Teacher

That small hand raised in my class
    today
  Is a sign of heart that was stirred.
Stirred by Your mighty Spirit, Lord
And the power of Your Holy Word.

That seed in a child's small heart,
    O Lord,
Is a fragile, tender thing.
But the soil is soft and workable
    Like a new-plowed field in spring.

How the devil would snatch and the
    world would press,
  Life's winds would whirl about,
On that tiny seed in the fertile earth.
  How can it ever hold out?

With a Sunday School teacher's deep
    love and tears,
  And with prayers rising up to God,
The devil himself can't keep those
    seeds
  From bursting through the sod!

          —*Ethel V. Leffel*

Retiring?

They say that you're retiring
  But that surely can't be true
For anyone who thinks you'll quit
  Knows not the pluck of you.
You've often labored long and lone
  To give each task your best
And no matter what the circumstance
  Passed "with honors" every test.

As onward now you swing into
  A little different stride
May each new day be filled with faith,
  With confidence and pride.
And should we ever forget your smile,
  Your words, or your cheerful nod,
The work of love you leave will
    stand—
  A monument to God.

          —*Florence Schufeldt*

Musings of a Bus Driver

I've looked at my route book, checked out every child;
It seems like today I may have quite a crowd.
There'll be Peter and Jimmy, with little sis Mae;
Their dad may be drunk while their mommy's away,
But they so love to ride in the Sunday School bus.
Even though they are dirty, and sometimes do cuss.
Jonathan's reg'lar. (I know all his jokes
But he sure likes to spring them on new little folks.)
There's Susan and Aaron, and sweet Betty Lou . . .
Dale, Howard, Mandy, Rebecca, and Sue . . .
Let's see . . . 42, 43, 46, (and I can't forget Kevin)
If they all come today, that will make 47.
Forty-seven? That can't be. For sure as I'm alive
God, You know my bus starts rocking when I've got just 35!

          —*Florence Schufeldt*

 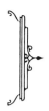

Of Interest to Women

Reflections

A Mother-Daughter Program

By Florence Harper Haney

Decorations

Place pastel-color candles in glass holders on mirror squares. Prepare silhouettes of mothers and daughters and mount in Styrofoam on opposite sides of vertical mirror squares. Use the mirrors, candles, and silhouettes throughout the room as desired.

Program

A Prayer for Mothers:

O God, we pray Your blessing on each mother here.
We thank You for their guidance year after year.

Grant strength to all young mothers, that is our prayer,
As they tend those babes and toddlers placed in their care.

A fever, a tumble, another night without rest.
Each day and each night seems to bring a new test:

As they soothe and they comfort their little ones, Lord,
May each mother, by Your love, feel herself restored.

Grant wisdom to the mature mothers, that too is our prayer;
As they counsel their youth in the problems they share.

Endless are the challenges of the growing-up years;
Fads and fashions, misunderstandings and tears.

As they teach and they guide these active ones, Lord,
May each mother, by Your love, feel herself restored.

Grant patience to the older mothers, that is our prayer;
As they face the slowing-down of life they must bear.

Memories mingle with today's deep emotion;
Children they've guided, now return their devotion.

As they lean on their sons and daughters, O Lord,
May each mother, by Your love, feel herself restored.

Hymn: "Since Jesus Came into My Life" *(First verse only.)*

Scripture Reading

Jesus said, "I am the light of the world: he that followeth me shall not walk in darkness, but shall have the light of life" (John 8:12). Jesus also said, "Ye are the light of the world. A city that is set on an hill cannot be hid. Neither do men light a candle, and put it under a bushel, but on a candlestick; and it giveth light unto all that are in the house. Let your light so shine before men, that they may see your good works, and glorify your Father which is in heaven" (Matthew 5:14-16).

Song: "This Little Light of Mine"

"Reflections of Three Generations"

Cast

NARRATOR
GRANDMOTHER
MOTHER   Not necessary to be actually related
DAUGHTER

Setting

The above three seated side by side at a long table. They face the audience. Each holds a hand mirror and has a candle before her. The candle in front of the grandmother is burning, the others are unlit.

NARRATOR—I look in a mirror and what do I see?
        The face in the reflection, is that really me?
        Sometimes the image seems to change and I think that I can see
        My mother's eyes, my daughter's smile, reflected back at me.
        It's true, our lives receive so much from one another:
        Daughter receives life and light from Grandmother and Mother.
        And all of us should reflect the love of God so full and free.
        Together let's say, "Allow Jesus' light shine each day through me."

GRANDMOTHER *(looks in her mirror)*—
        The day I first became a mother,
          Is the day I will never forget.
        The days and years I spent with my child
          Were even sweeter yet.
        I didn't think I could share love
          And happiness with another.
        But my joy is multiplied now.
          Because I am a grandmother.
           (Pause.)
I have a light in my soul that Jesus gave me!
It was from *my* mother I first learned He came to save me.

Through childhood years, in good times and bad,
She shared my laughter when I was happy; my tears when I was sad.

She taught me how to cook and sew—and, oh, so many things!
But most of all, she shared with me the light that Jesus brings.

16

This light that came from my dear mother, so many years ago,
I pass it now to you. There's no greater gift a mother can bestow.

(Grandmother lights the candle of Mother from her candle.)

MOTHER *(looks in her mirror)*—

I open each lovely card on Mother's Day,
And tears fill my eyes when I read what they say.

My children choose verses of sweet love and praise,
That thank me for understanding their puzzling ways.

I thank You, God, that my children understand me,
And saw through my faults, the mother I tried to be.

Someday I think I'll put Mother's Day in reverse,
And give my children praise in sweet, loving verse.
(Pause.)

This light and mirror both remind me what joy my memory brings.
My mother and my children have given me such wonderful things.

I remember how my mother prayed as she knelt beside my small bed.
"God bless this little child of mine. Help me teach her Your ways," she
said.

I can think of many things I did that made her worry and cry.
Yes, there were doubts, questions, disagreements, that did her patience try.

But her prayers were many, and her faith was so strong, her love so deep,
That I know God's ways I learned as a child were the ways I wanted to
keep.

She passed to me the light that Jesus gave her. It's what makes life worth
living,
This precious light of love and grace, to you now, my child I am giving.

(Mother lights the candle of Daughter from her candle.)

DAUGHTER *(looks in her mirror)*—

If you asked me to show you a picture of love,
I wouldn't have far to look.
I wouldn't go to a museum.
Or search through an artist's book.

I'd just say, Come home with me,
There are some people I want you to see
Have a talk with my mother,
And then come meet my grandmother.

All you'd ever want to know
About love shows in the way their lives glow.
(Pause.)

In the mirror and the shining light, we find a message that lives.
We all need each other to help pass along the grace that Jesus gives.

My path from here, I do not know. The future in darkness hides.
But I need not fear with Grandmother and Mother as my guides.

They have taught me to know that Jesus cares about everything I do.
And I see in their lives that what they teach is beautiful and true.

As the years go by in Jesus' care, I will listen and I will learn
How to live for Him each day, for soon it will be my turn

To lift this light high, that I received from my mother,
And joyfully pass its message of love on to another.

Hymn: "Pass It On"

Fashions

A Mother-Daughter Banquet Program

By Cora M. Owen

Table Centerpieces

Use dolls of appropriate size dressed in different fashions. You may wish to use fashions of the past or of other lands. Dolls may be borrowed from a collector or from local children.

Place Cards

Cut colored construction paper into 3 x 5" rectangles. Fold in half so they will stand. Sew or glue varicolored buttons and small bows to the paper. Hand-letter names. Teens may wish to help you with this project. Decorations should carry out the buttons and bows theme.

Fashion Show

Plan a small fashion show composed of local women in fashions of another era. It may be interesting to have daughters wear their mothers' wedding gowns. You may wish to award prizes for various categories.

Readings

The following are a series of readings that underscore the fashions theme—"God's Fashions." It is for a leader and six women or girls.

God's Fashions

Leader: Each year a list of the 10 best-dressed women is compiled by the world's fashion designers. Those who have the financial means are thrilled to be chosen for this honor. Women of high social standing long for the privilege of being so named. We may never be selected for such commendation, but the subject of wearing apparel is of importance to most of us.

The age-old question is still worth considering: do we follow the current fashion trends or do we retain our own individuality? If one doesn't conform, she may look strange and out of step. Those who design feminine apparel are always looking for something new. The fashion industry depends upon hem lines raising and lowering. It's a form of planned obsolescence.

There is, however, a world of attire where things never change; where the raiment never becomes old-fashioned or outdated. The Great Designer of this array is God himself. He has provided the most attractive clothing available for every Christian girl and woman. This finery is not costly, but it is given as a free gift to all who will take it and wear it.

First Reader: (Read Isaiah 61:10.) The first item that God has patterned is the garment of salvation. This is cut from the most beautiful of materials, the cloth of *love*. Only He could provide such a perfect outfit. It is possible for you to wear this lovely gown because of Christ's sacrificial death on Calvary. By faith in Him, the garment of salvation is received. It will never deteriorate or lose its value. It was purchased for you to keep forever.

Second Reader: (Read Isaiah 61:10.) Another article of exquisite clothing is found in the same verse—it too speaks of originals. Its lines are soft and formed from the fabric of His grace. When you have put on the robe of righteousness, all the rags of sin and self-righteousness will be exchanged for His righteousness. You will be radiant in this superb costume for all eternity.

Third Reader: (Read Isaiah 61:3.) A most desirable type of covering, is the Great Originator's garment of praise. This creation is modeled after the angel's songs. It is woven from music, harmony, and glory to God. It comes from the heart made glad because of His goodness and mercy. This garment is embroidered with the threads of rejoicing. Its delicate texture will endure.

Fourth Reader: (Read Ephesians 6:15.) Before going out for a special occasion, you as a fashion-conscious young lady, will secure the proper shoes. You will be sure to have footwear that is stylish, well-fitting, and comfortable. The Creator of the perfect ensemble has provided suitable shoes for the feet of those who walk with Him. "Your feet shod with the preparation of the gospel of peace." When wearing these shoes, you will be prompt and ready to spread good tidings of God's peace. Your steps will be sure and firm. You will tread the paths of peace directed by the God of Peace. Your shoes will never wear out.

Fifth Reader: (Read 1 Peter 3:4.) As a well-dressed woman, you would not think your outfit complete without the proper accessories. They must compliment your outfit in color and design. They must glow with elegance and charm. God's fashions include jewelry; not outward adornments, but the "ornament of a meek and quiet spirit." This is an inner beauty which you will reflect outwardly. Your countenance and character will manifest Christ dwelling within you. God says this kind of ornament is of great value in His sight. These accessories will never rust or tarnish.

Sixth Reader: (Read Isaiah 59:17.) To cover your splendid attire, you must have the most suitable garment available. God has given you the cloak of zeal. Without enthusiasm in serving, your work for Him will not prosper. He gives you warmth and an ardor. He gives you an avid interest in working for His cause. He will wrap you in the spotless folds of this great cloak, and will cause you to be fruitful for Him. The fabric of this covering will never unravel.

Leader: Your garb is now complete, and you are ready to make your appearance in society as a servant of God.

The importance of fashion should not be underrated. If you are one who is attractively dressed, you will be assured and self-confident. You will have the poise that is necessary in order to succeed in today's world.

Yet, with all the assurance, poise, and self-confidence that materialistic and worldly fashion can provide, it is well to remember that these qualities are fleeting. The spiritual blessings of God's gifts of fashions will outlast all the sparkling array of contemporary style. In the ever-changing realm of style, the most costly, original outfit will soon be outmoded. In His infinite wisdom God has shaped the most chic wardrobe imaginable. It is available at no cost. It is made up of materials which are indestructable. Let Him weave the fabrics' warp and woof of love and grace. Let Him array you in the finest textured garments.

Go to the Master Designer for a wardrobe which is most artistic in flair and style. Then you can be sure of apparel that is always well fitting, well made, proper, and becoming.

Salute to Nursery Workers

For all the times you had to listen to a choir of crying babies;
   We salute you!
For letting them pull your hair, muss your clothing, and cut their teeth on your hand or leg;
   We salute you!
For all the special attention you've given to our babies; for all the crackers you have distributed; for all the bottles you have warmed; for all the diapers you have changed;
   We salute you!
Today, as we honor you, our nursery attendants, we thank you for showing God's love to our wee ones, and for exercising patience in a way that would have impressed Job himself. We pray that God will bless and give you a deep feeling of satisfaction for your tireless work. [List names.]
   We salute you today!

—*Martha Bolton*

Times of Remembrance

We Must Move On

Memorial Service

By Grace Ramquist

Directions for Presentation:

In preparation for the reading of the Memoirs report, the organist softly plays "Still, Still with Thee." Without introduction, the Reader and Soloist take their places on the platform. As the music fades, the Soloist sings stanzas four and five of the above hymn. At close of song, the organist continues to play softly while the Reader prepares to read.

Organist *(softly playing):* "Still, Still with Thee"

Soloist *(stanzas four and five):* "Still, Still with Thee"

Reader *(while Organist continues to play):*

In some ways life in the church is like the moving of the earth. Even though the earth constantly moves on its axis, we people are unaware of its movement except as scientists report it to us. Nevertheless the earth does move! In fact it never stops.

So it is with the church. The people of the church keep moving. Age-wise, that is. Our little ones join the nursery; They quietly pass to toddler. It seems such a short time and they are in kindergarten, then primary, middler, junior, high school. The years pass and "we who belong together" keep moving on.

Today we are remembering those who took their last moves on earth this past year. Somehow we expected them to be with us always.

A total of _____ members were taken in death this year. We remember _____ (tell of the relationship to the church family.) Our loss of _____ was surely heaven's gain. *(Continue with the list of names. If time permits, the relationship and place of service may be mentioned. Be sure all information is written and nothing is spoken ad lib.)*

Many of our number have suffered the loss of beloved relatives, not members of our congregation. These we tenderly remember.

21

God's plan for the earth does not allow it to stop moving; and neither can we as a church. Let us pledge to each other we will keep our hearts full of love for God and determine to be faithful to the end.

"For a thousand years in the sight of God are but as yesterday when it is past, and as a watch in the night."

". . . we spend our years as a tale that is told."

"For none of us liveth to himself, and no man dieth to himself.

"For whether we live, we live unto the Lord; and whether we die, we die unto the Lord: whether we live therefore, or die, we are the Lord's."

And now, dear Lord,

"So teach us to number our days, that we may apply our hearts unto wisdom."

We pray Thee:

". . . Let the beauty of the Lord our God be upon us: and establish thou the work of our hands upon us; yea, the work of our hands establish thou it."

Prayer: Minister

Poppies of the Field

Memorial Service

By Grace Ramquist

Directions for Presenting
When the memorial service is to begin, the Organist (or pianist) starts softly playing "O Jesus, I Have Promised." At the close of the playing, the Soloist or group of Singers step to the microphone and sing the first and third stanzas of the same hymn. At the conclusion of singing, the Reader quickly takes his or her place at the microphone and reads. In the script below, where the blanks appear, names of those deceased are added. If the Reader wishes to add some short statement concerning one or more persons, these words should be written and added to the script before the service. Any extemporaneous words will take away from the beauty and solemnity of the service.

Organist—"O Jesus, I Have Promised"

Soloist—"O Jesus, I Have Promised" *(stanzas one and three)*

Reader—Man . . . cometh forth like a flower . . .
As a flower of the field, so he flourisheth—
. . . the flower fadeth—
. . . the wind passeth over it, and it is gone.

It was morning early in the spring. When the front door was opened the miracle of a field of poppies was revealed. The flowers rhythmically moved their heads in the wind. Their bright orange color could be seen by all who passed. Many stopped to gaze upon their beauty.

They brought beauty, hope, and praise to the hearts of the passersby. As the days passed, they continued to hold high their heads, but their color faded a bit, a petal was dropped here and there, until one morning, the field of poppies was no more.

Even though they were gone, the place where they had stood so proudly, seemed to keep a part of their beauty. Sometimes the heads of passersby turned toward where the flowers had waved so beautifully.

Today, as I stand before you, in my mind's eye I can see those who have lived and gone. There have been numerous relatives and friends who were here but a short year ago. There were aunts, uncles, mothers, fathers, grandmothers, grandmothers, and children—all relatives of those who remain.

Each person here remembers certain pews in the church sanctuary where departed members once sat. If we close our eyes we can see them as "poppies of the field" of heaven, waving their heads in the breezes of that new forever land.

We remember: _____, _____.

It would be impossible to forget _____ and _____-
_____.

(Other names are to be added. Each name should be read with feeling for each person who has passed from this life during the year is important to someone in your audience.)

Not only were these our friends and loved ones faithful until death, but with confidence we know they are standing with the redeemed of the Lord, their heads held high, happily rejoicing in the knowledge they have fought a good fight and have kept the faith.

Man . . . cometh forth like a flower—
As a flower of the field, so he flourisheth,
. . . the flower fadeth.
. . . the wind passeth over it, and it is gone.
For those who have been faithful, Jesus gave a promise.

"In my Father's house are many mansions . . . I will . . . receive you unto myself; that where I am, there ye may be also."

Prayer—Minister

I Shall Be like Him

Memorial Service

By Grace Ramquist

Directions for Presentation:
While the Soloist and Reader are taking their places on the platform, the Organist softly plays "I Shall Be like Him." Before the ending of the song playing, the Soloist takes her place at the microphone and is ready to sing when the last notes die away. The Organist may continue to play during the reading, if the audience can hear over the music.

Organist *(plays softly):* "I Shall Be like Him"

Soloist: "I Shall Be like Him"

Reader *(stepping to platform and microphone as Soloist takes his or her seat):*

> All their lives, Christians
> Seek to be more like Jesus.
>
> Shortcomings plague man—
> Oh, so many mistakes are made;
> Countless sorrows are suffered;
> Hosts of disappointments come
> And burdens—too heavy to bear alone.
>
> There are tears—
> Tears of pain,
> Tears of compassion,
> Tears of anxiety,
> Tears of remorse,
> Tears of loneliness.
>
> Then at last, comes the day
> of sweet release.
> All sorrows are past,
> All tears are gone forever.
>
> We have seen friends
> Wipe tears from the eyes of a beloved;
> But in that blessed land, not
> A friend and not an angel,
> But God himself wipes away
> All tears from His children's eyes.
> God takes away all reasons for tears.

24

All is well for
There is no more death,
Neither sorrow,
Nor crying.

Neither pain,
For the former things are passed away.
God says, "Behold, I make all things new.
"I will give unto him that is athirst
    of the fountain of life freely.
"He that overcometh shall inherit all things;
    and I will be his God, and he shall be my son."

Today we are remembering
Those who finished their days on earth
During the past year.

They are:
*(List them and read each name carefully. Remember
everyone is very important to his family.)*

As we sit together here today
We know these of our number are
Enjoying a new, glorious life.
More and more they will grow like Him.
More and more they will see things as they are.

"More and more like Him repeat the blest story,
Over and over again!
Changed by His Spirit from glory to glory,
I shall be satisfied then."

Congregation *(softly sings refrain):* "I Shall Be like Him"

Prayer: Minister

Who Healeth

Memorial Service

By Grace Ramquist

Directions for Presentation:
    Organist softly plays "God Will Take Care of You" as Soloist and Reader take their places on the platform. As the last strains of the music come to an end, the Soloist steps to the platform microphone and sings. The Reader takes his or her place as soon as Soloist is seated.

Organist *(softly plays):* "God Will Take Care of You"

Soloist *(stepping to microphone sings):* "God Will Take Care of You"

Reader *(stepping to microphone and speaking either with soft music accompaniment or without it):* All who were left of the family were gathered in the living room borrowed from friends. It has been a sad day, for the body of the mother was lying in the mortuary a few blocks away awaiting the funeral on the coming day.
    All present knew the father minister was suffering even as if his body had been sawn in two. When he was but 18 years of age, he and the deceased had been married. They had loved, they had suffered, they had been happy, they had been sad, they had dreamed together for 37 years.
    The family had been a close one and as they sat around the room, each member silently was remembering days gone by. Reaching into his pocket, the father drew out his Bible. He turned the pages until he came to the Psalms.
    "I am going to read your mother's favorite psalm," he said. And then he read,
    "Bless the Lord, O my soul: and all that is within me, bless his holy name."
    Before the mind's eye of one daughter sat the little black-haired mother. She remembered that during all of her life, frequently during each day, her mother had burst out in praise to God with the words being read. The father continued reading:
    "Bless the Lord, O my soul, and forget not all his benefits."
    "Who forgiveth all thine iniquities; who healeth all thy diseases."
    He stopped reading. In a firm, but quiet voice, he spoke. "He has healed all your mother's diseases."
    The room was quiet for a moment. The mother had never been what one might call husky, although she had worked hard all her life. All knew she had sicknesses about which she rarely spoke. As her life flashed before

those left, there came a sudden joy. How wonderful! She was now healed! No more sickness. Forever.

The father went ahead reading the rest of the psalm. Very few of the words made an impression on the group for somehow their thoughts stayed on the words, "Who healeth all thy diseases."

Today as we remember those of our number who have departed this life, each of us can remember some diseases from which one or two of our deceased members have now been healed. Doctors do their best, yet there comes a time when after everything humanly possible has been done, the good Lord above takes over. It is He who has the power to heal diseases. He heals cancer; He heals sick hearts; He heals nervous disorders; He heals any and all.

We remember _____. (List those who have departed during the year. If desirous and time permits, names and positions held in the church may be recalled. Be sure everything to be read is written down and before you.)

There are many of our group who have lost mothers, fathers, sisters, and brothers, uncles and aunts, grandmothers and grandfathers, and friends dear to their hearts. These, too, we remember.

With me, listen to the words:

"Bless the Lord, O my soul; and all that is within me, bless his holy name.

"Bless the Lord, O my soul, and forget not all his benefits.

"Who forgiveth all thine iniquities; who health all thy diseases:

"Who redeemeth thy life from destruction; who crowneth thee with lovingkindness and tender mercies.

"Who satisfieth thy mouth with good things; so that thy youth is renewed like the eagle's.

"The Lord hath prepared his throne in the HEAVENS:

"O Lord my God, thou art very great; thou art clothed with honor and majesty."

Prayer: Minister

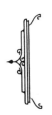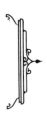

Promoting the Program

You Probably Don't Remember Me

Dear Sunday School Teachers:
You probably don't remember me.
I was one of many little girls
    who attended your Sunday school classes.
I came to you dressed in dotted swiss
          and patent leather
    looking like somebody's little darling,
    but sincerely wishing I were
          somewhere, anywhere else.
I squirmed and fidgeted during your
    story of Noah,
        and said I didn't care why
God sent the Flood; I wanted
        my daddy.

In junior high
    I was the one who passed notes to Mark
        under the table;
    the one who tricked Julie into reading
        the seventh chapter of Solomon's Song
    for a Sunday School devotional;
    the one who insisted you explain
        (in front of the whole class)
    whom Jesus would decide to save
    if two people were drowning.
I was the one in the college class
        (just before I dropped out)
    who asked you, as you spoke of
        God's unconditional love,
    if it really mattered anyway,
        since rumor had it
          God was dead.

But one dreadful night, dear teachers,
 my world crashed in around me.
Fear and bitterness and depression
  threatened to push me across that fine line
  that separates the rational from the
    otherwise.
In my utter desperation I cried out to the God
  you had assured me existed.
I begged Him to rescue me from myself.
    To save me.
   To show me the way to Him.

Jesus responded to me, dear teachers,
  through a verse you so patiently prodded me
  to memorize one Sunday, as I squirmed
   and fidgeted in my
    dotted swiss.
"I am the way, the truth, and the life.
No man cometh unto the Father, except by me."

He comforted me during that long, lonely night
  as I repeated those precious verses
  you taught me year after year.
The truth and strength of those passages provided
  a lifeline at the end of my rope,
  a footbridge across that terrifying chasm
   between darkness and light.

You probably don't remember me,
  dear Sunday School teachers,
   but I remember you.

How eternally grateful I will be for
  your patience
  your persistence
  and your love.

How sorry I am that I have lost track of you,
  and can't come to you and hug you,
  and share with you my glorious
   (though belated) discovery that
    He lives!
    and
    He loves me!
Just like you said
   all along.

       —Shannon J. White

Bible, Best-seller

(An exercise for 12 children)

1st Child—My dad says that the Bible is the most valuable Book in the world. That's why it is a best-seller.

2nd Child—Most other books that are best-sellers are popular for only a short time, but the Bible has been read and loved for centuries, and by people of many countries.

3rd Child—I know that most of the great men of our country have valued the Bible. George Washington said, "It is impossible to rightly govern the world without God and the Bible. He is worse than an infidel who does not read his Bible."

4th Child—Our second president, John Adams, wrote, "The Bible is the best Book in the world." He read a chapter from the Book every day.

5th Child—Thomas Jefferson, who wrote our Declaration of Independence, loved his Bible and read it. From him came the words, "I have always said that the study of this sacred volume will make better citizens and better fathers. The Bible makes the best people in the world."

6th Child—At one time Lincoln said, "I am profitably engaged in reading the Bible. It is God's best gift to man."

7th Child—Our more recent presidents were of the same opinion. In New England you may be shown a spot in the woods where Theodore Roosevelt often used to go to quietly read the Bible. His sister, in writing about him, tells us that he knew a great deal of Scripture by memory.

8th Child—The later President Roosevelt, Franklin Delano Roosevelt, declared, "If men and nations would return to the teachings of the Sermon on the Mount, there would not be all these troubled times in the world today."

9th Child—Woodrow Wilson, who was president of a university before he was president of our country, said, "No one is really educated who is not familiar with the Bible."
President Herbert Hoover wrote, "To read the Bible is a necessity of American life."

10th Child—We have all heard about Douglas McArthur who helped win the war with Japan and later was head of the army group which went into Japan to aid them in recovering from the effects of the war. With all these great responsibilities, he has told us, "Believe me, never a night goes by, be I ever so tired, but I read the Word of God before I go to bed."

11th Child—Most of us know about Captain Rickenbacker and how he was afloat in a small life raft for many days upon the empty vastness of the Pacific Ocean. Afterward he said, "Probably I would not have survived if it had not been for the strength I received from the Bible."

12th Child—"All scripture is given by inspiration of God, and is profitable for doctrine, for reproof, for correction, for instruction in righteousness:
"That the man of God may be perfect, throughly furnished unto all good works" (2 Timothy 3:16-17).

—*Daisy Jenney Clay*

Masks

(Installation of officers)

EQUIPMENT:

Four masks made of construction paper attached to handles. Paint a smile on one, a wink on one, a frown on one, and one with both eyes shut. Each mask should be presented by the officer doing the installing, who speaks the prepared charge.

Charge

SMILING MASK—As president of this organization you will have a lot to smile about. But more important are the smiles you will bring to others. We trust you will serve with a happy heart.

WINKING MASK—As vice-president, this winking mask will serve to remind you of how much work you must do in a wink. At times you will be called upon to substitute for the president, so get a good grip on yourself and enjoy this honor shown you.

FROWNING MASK—As secretary, I hope you will have little reason to frown. If you keep your records up to date you'll turn this frown upside down and always have a happy face.

EYES SHUT MASK—Your mask has its eyes shut, but we know you will keep your eyes wide open as you serve as treasurer of this fine organization. Your office is one of great trust and responsibility.

DEDICATORY PLEDGE *(new officers in unison)*—We pledge our loyalty, zeal, honesty, and integrity to the _____ organization. We will do our best in the year ahead to uphold the principles and values of our offices.

DEDICATORY PRAYER—Lord, we ask Your blessings upon each of these who have been installed this night. We pray that You will guide, strengthen, and undergird them. We pray for this organization and each of its members. In Jesus' name. Amen.

—*Gean D. Smith*

Choir Rehearsal

It happened at a meeting when an organ key got stuck;
The organist got hysterics and the director ran amuck.
The song books fell a-clattering, causing havoc in the choir;
The sopranos started singing lower and the basses going higher.
The pianist who was snoozing started playing, thinking it time to go;
The altos started singing faster and the tenors singing slow.
The preacher started saying, "Making a joyful noise is not a sin";
The choir just kept on singing and the deacons said, "Amen."
So, if you fancy yourself a singer or if you so aspire;
Just feel free at any time to come and join our choir.

—*Gean D. Smith*

Salute to Sunday School Workers

Thank you, teachers, for your labors
    With the children in our town;
Hours of study, faithful visits,
    Carving jewels for Christ's crown!

You have prayed and interceded;
    You have taught the Holy Word;
From your lips we've learned of Jesus;
    In your life, we've seen the Lord!

You have listened, you have
        counseled;
    Spiritual victories have been won!
Thank you, teachers, for your efforts;
    May God bless you, every one!

—Anna Marie Dahlquist

Promotion Day

We've reached a brand-new milestone,
    We've come a long, long way!
We're ready for new classes
    On this promotion day!

But the honor and the credit
    Must be given where it is due;
Thanks go to our teachers and parents,
    And our Heavenly Father too!

We've reached a brand-new milestone,
    But we have just begun
A new lap in our journey,
    So pray for us, each one!

—Anna Marie Dahlquist

A Charge to Sunday School Workers

You makers of mosaics in lives—
    Take from your artist's chest
The tools of God's Word, the gems of
        truth,
    The brightest and the best.

The child knows not the bright design
    You patiently intend;
But don't give up, for line on line,
    He'll profit in the end.

Work on; place carefully each piece;
    A lesson on God's care,
Or one on God's laws, another on
        grace,
    And one on how to share.

When every.piece is where you've
        planned,
    And a wholesome balance is
        brought,
He will be grateful to the hands
    Which his life's mosaics have
        wrought.

—Anna Marie Dahlquist

Days of Celebration

Engagement Party or Wedding Shower

By Esther M. Bailey

(Bake two angel food cakes, slice off a section of each, place together and frost. Before cutting the cake, the following speech should be given by the hostess or emcee.)

As this cake is used to celebrate the engagement of _____ and _____, it is symbolic in many ways.

First of all, the *kind* of cake tells us something: angel food cake. In contracting for a marriage, Christians do more than buy a ring, send out invitations, and arrange for the services of a photographer. For the Christian, negotiations with heaven are even more important than the necessary preparations for the wedding day. When the divine plan of marriage becomes reality in personal lives, a sort of fellowship with angels results. Indeed, at this wonderful time in their lives, I dare say that *(first names only)* feel as though God had dispatched an entire band of angels to perform an earthly mission on their behalf.

Two separate cakes were used to fashion a likeness to the double wedding rings. One cake is inscribed with _____'s name, the other one with _____'s name, representing two lives that will soon merge into one. In order to create the quality of oneness, it was necessary to slice off a portion of each cake. That's how a beautiful marriage relationship works. Each person discards certain aspects of individuality in favor of a more perfect blending of the two personalities. By giving up one small segment of self, the potential for life's blessings is doubled as two people share experiences ranging from happiness to disappointment.

Finally, the two cakes lost individual identity when a mountain of white fluffy frosting joined them together. This symbolizes the marriage ceremony, ordained by God, intended to preserve the marital relationship. As *(first names only)* are soon to make their pledge of permanent commitment to each other, let us pray that they may realize all that God has in store for them. *(Prays or calls on someone else to pray.)*

Graduation

Graduation is many-colored—
   Kaleidoscopic memories of the past
A tinge of gold
   for today's achievement
Bright blues of faith and hope
   for all the tomorrows.
May you let God weave these
   into a tapestry
    worthy of His workmanship—
A life of continuing beauty
   and of joy in service.

—Florence Schufeldt

Dedication of a Baby

Lord, thank You for this precious little baby;
    Lovingly nurtured, tenderly wrapped, so new!
It's with great joy we gather here together
    To dedicate this little life to You.

Just as a tender rosebud in the morning
    Lifts to the sun its petals covered with dew,
So may this little heart early open to Jesus—
    This little life we dedicate to You.

We see our pastor place his hand of blessing
    Upon the infant head, and we pray with him too,
"Lord, place *Your* hand on the baby and on the parents,
    And bless the lives we dedicate to You!"

—Anna Marie Dahlquist

For the Christian Bride

Begin each day with Christ, alone in earnest prayer;
Rejoice in everything together as God lifts each care.
Intermingle common sense and love throughout your life to-
    gether, and all your
Discussions will be pleasant times, as welcome as sunny
    weather. Our
Earnest wish today is in this little prayer, that God will keep
    you and your husband within His loving care.

—June Jester

For a Wedding Anniversary

Our God has granted you these years together;
    You've shared both sorrow and life's full delight,
You've seen God meet your needs as you have trusted;
    Prayer has become thanksgiving; faith is sight.

As you have kept, still keep first joy in Jesus,
    Let His sweet words your deepest love beget;
Keep trusting Him in every situation,
    And you will find your heart's desires still met.

We'll thank the Lord for all the days behind you,
    And trust His grace for every day ahead;
He will provide, as always He's provided,
    And He will lead, as always He has led.

—Anna Marie Dahlquist

For the Dedication of a House

Dear Lord, with grateful heart
  We give this house° to Thee
And purpose that its every part
  To Thee shall honoring be.

May these Thy walls never ring
  With selfish, dull complaints,
Or idle gossip's deadly sting,
  Or foolish arguments.

But let the sweet perfume
  Of love pervade the air;
Breathe into each and every room
  An atmosphere of prayer.

Dear Lord, with grateful heart,
  We give this house to Thee,
That to Thyself its every part
  May glorifying be.

      —*Anna Marie Dahlquist*

°The word *building* may be substituted.

50th Wedding Anniversary

God hasn't always given you
  A smooth and easy road,
But He was there with love and care
  To lighten every load.

And He has walked beside you
  In bright sunshine and in showers,
And here and there around the bend
  A bright bouquet of flowers.

He's blessed your home with children
  You've laughed and worked and
    played.
For 50 years God's never failed
  He's listened when you prayed.

And so we wish for you our best
  And love for all your days.
Confident that God will grant
  Bright moments filled with praise.

That each new day will echo back
  To those sweet wedding bells!
We wish you peace, we wish you joy,
  Dear friends, we wish you well!

      —*Ethel V. Leffel*

An Anniversary Tribute

When God planned marriage, I wonder if He had in mind,
(First names) as examples for all of mankind.
Perhaps He knew what a team they would be
And He said,"That's what I call a family."

So on (month, day, and year) this man and woman were wed.
"I now pronounce you husband and wife," the preacher said.
Their lives had been two; now they were one,
Rich with assurance that God's will had been done.

For _____ years they've walked hand in hand,
Building a family, spreading love throughout the land.
They're committed to God in body and soul,
Pointing the way to heaven is their ultimate goal.

So if the _____ were God's prototype of wedded bliss,
I'm sure He, too, is celebrating at a time like this.
And as _____ pays them tribute in song
Perhaps the angels in heaven will sing along.

      —*Esther M. Bailey*

Recipe for a Happy Marriage

Line your marriage with solid devotion to God,
Laced with genuine respect for each other.
Season it with a sense of high adventure.
Over all pour the milk of loving kindness
    and the oil of forgiveness.
Garnish it with a generous dash of humor.
Bake for a lifetime
In the warmth of God's understanding, unfailing love.

—Florence Schufeldt

A Wish
For a Wedding Anniversary

May your anniversary be
    Just as glad as when you wed,
As you gladly think about
    How you met, what you said.

And may all the road ahead,
    As the days, unfolding, bloom
Into months and years, still be
    An unceasing honeymoon.

—Anna Marie Dahlquist

Values

Eternal values are not won
    By good deeds done or honors sung,
But by the heart of God made glad
    By what we did with what we had!

—Florence Schufeldt

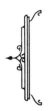

In Praise of Babies

Baby Talk

A Baby Celebration

By Zeta Combs Davidson

The following are ideas for a shower or celebration for a mother-to-be. Portions of this material may be used effectively as features in a service to honor babies and their parents.

INVITATION

If you *talk* to ___(honored guest's name)___, she will tell you that the ___(couple's last name)___ _____ are having a baby. Please come to honor her (them) on ___(date)___ at ___(time)___. We will be *talk*ing *baby* at ___(location)___. You may find yourself *talk*ing *baby talk*, who knows?

> Hostesses
> RSVP information

DECORATIONS

Arrange a child's table and chairs for a tea party with dolls and stuffed animals. Toy telephones and/or other talking toys grouped together for a table centerpiece (pretty with fresh flowers).

GIFT SUGGESTIONS

To fit the theme, suggest gifts that "talk" or communicate a message. Here are a few ideas:
   Baby book
   Christian Mother Goose
   Pink or blue New Testament imprinted with the new baby's name
   Child's talking toy
   Musical crib mobile

ACTIVITIES

Baby Talk Game for New Mothers

Suggest to the guest of honor that she will have to learn to interpret baby talk, and that this game will indeed help her get started. For added fun, discover some of the favorite baby talk phrases of toddlers in your own church. Add them to this list (with baby's name, of course). On the line following the baby talk phrase, write the correct interpretation.

1. Write dare _____
2. Red ego _____
3. Fish flies _____
4. Ma'am aw _____
5. Tote awn _____
6. Nigh nigh _____
7. Aw sh-h jews _____
8. Bank E _____
9. O. P. Door _____
10. Ah me nit _____
11. Pap paw _____
12. We weed _____
13. Wad doer _____
14. Pod E _____

ANSWERS:
1. Right there
2. (I'm) ready (to) go
3. French fries
4. Grandma
5. (Put my) coat on
6. (I want to go) nighty night
7. Orange juice
8. Blanket
9. Open (the) door
10. I mean it
11. Grandpa
12. Read, read
13. Water
14. Potty

Birthday Letter

Have persons in the group supply responses to the following questions. As someone reads the form "letter" fill in the blanks from your own list of responses. This may be used in a humorous way at a shower, or in a serious vein as a gift to a child on his or her birthday.

1. Name of child _____
2. Age _____
3. Event from past year _____
4. Desired quality of life _____
5. Gift from God _____
6. Age _____
7. Parent's hope for child _____
8. A happening (present or future) _____
9. Thought or feeling _____
10. Lesson about God taught by parents _____
11. Unhappy or hurtful event _____
12. Happy occasion or successful event _____
13. Discouraging happening _____
14. Age _____
15. Author of letter _____

You may wish to duplicate the following letter, and allow guest to fill in the blanks.

Dear Child of Mine:

Today, _____(1)_____, you are _____(2)_____. During this past year, your daddy (mother) and I have watched you as _____(3)_____ _____(4)_____. We've waited to see you _____(5)_____. We realize that God has given you _____(6)_____. Our hope for you, now that you are ___(7)___, is that _____(8)_____. Together we've planned _____(9)_____. Our thoughts and feelings have been _____(10)_____. We want you to know God's love, and have tried to show you the Way by _____(11)_____. We really did hurt for you when _____(12)_____. We rejoiced with you when you _____(13)_____. We allowed you to _____(14)_____ _____ because we know this can be a step in God's plan for your life. Our prayer is that God will show us what part He wants us to have in your life now that you are ___(15)___ today.

Love,

_____

FOR A DEVOTIONAL

TALK TO ME—MY MOTHER

You may wish to consider "writing" this letter every year, starting with the year a child is born. This will become a wonderful birthday keepsake and record of the child's development.

Talk to me—my mother,
  Tell me all the things you know;
So when I grow to be a man,
  My Father's love will show.

Talk to me—my mother,
  Tell me how the world was made;
So when I look about the land,
  I'll know whose plan was laid.

Talk to me—my mother,
  Read me Bible tales of old;
They will be example
  Of the Way, as they are told.

Talk to me—my mother,
  Hold me close and give me of
The tender care you know so well,
  That truly shows God's love.

Talk to me—my mother,
  Tell me why you think and feel
His plan is so important
  To build a life that's real!

Talk to me—my mother,
  Show me how to live a life;
That pleases God in all I do—
  And comforts those in strife.

Talk to me—my mother,
  Share ideas of how to be
The person in the Christian life
  Who God says, "Pleases me."

Talk to me—my mother,
  Tell me all the things you know;
So when I grow to be a man,
  My Father's love will show.

A "Baby Day" Display

By Sharon Miller

Cover a table with a soft yellow cloth (a sheet will do). Drape light green nylon net around it in swags. At the swag points, put a cluster of artificial spring flowers and ribbon streamers.

Divide the table into three areas and place in each, objects that represent a specific area of growth: physical, mental, and spiritual. The symbolic objects might be:

Physical growth—Baby food bottles, milk bottle, ball, photo album of young child from birth to four years.

Mental growth—Blocks, books, an educational toy, and an adult book about early learning.

Spiritual growth—Small church, Bible, copies of children's Bible story books.

Prepare three signs: "A Baby Grows Physically," "A Baby Grows Mentally," "A Baby Grows Spiritually." Place these placards with appropriate displays on the table. On a bulletin board adjacent to the table, arrange photos of the church's babies. You may wish to distribute information about the church's Cradle Roll program, nursery facilities and workers, and a family devotional book.

Questionings of a Mother

(A Soliloquy)

The Baby Years
  Are sleepless nights and frustrating
    days more than compensated
    when our children say, "I love
    you"?
  Will spankings, scoldings, hugging,
    and comforting help them to
    grow into responsible adults?
  Can trips to the park, rides on a
    merry-go-round, picnics, and
    mountain hikes, or splashing in a
    wading pool and birthday
    presents insure them a happy life?
  Does church school, prayer, and
    Bible-reading, examples of
    honesty and good living give
    faith in God?
The Baby Years
  When character begins its
    development.
  Could the most important thing we
    give them be the knowledge of
    how much we love them?

—*Grace Richie*

To a Newborn Child

God has sent you down from heavenly
    places
  To bring to earth innocence and
    love;
  To add to the joy and testing of
    family life;
  To fulfill a special need
    and a special place
    in the world.
  To be an opportunity for new
    beginnings;
  To act as an instrument for the
    hands of God.
Welcome, little one, to this, our world.

—*Grace Richie*

Tell Your Children

(Church anniversary, dedication)

Grace Hawthorne

Tom Fettke

Firmly
Unison

1. God the Fa - ther, God in — glo - ry,— Mir - a - cles and mys - ter-
2. Lift the fal - len, feed the— hun - gry;— God pro -vides for ev - 'ry -
3. Awe in - spir - ing deeds of— splen-dor,— These pro-claim His might - y

y; Gen - er - a - tions all a - dore— Him; God, the same through
thing. He is fair and full of kind - ness; Gen - er - a - tions
pow'r; In - ter - wo - ven with com - pas - sion, Give us strength for

Parts

his - to - ry.
prais - es sing. Par - ents tell— your chil - dren;
ev - 'ry hour.

Age to age— the same. Glo - ri - fy the liv - ing Lord a-bove, Mag-ni-

fy His ho - ly— name, mag-ni - fy His ho - ly— name.

Don't Be Afraid, Little Children

F. W. H.
(Babies or children emphasis)
Floyd W. Hawkins

All Your Life
(Graduation)

Bless This House

(Church dedication)

R. K.

Robert Kircher

vo - tion,_____ Their bod - ies weak, yet strong in love of

Thee._____ Bless Thou the minds who pressed with stead - fast____

spir - it _____ A - gainst all trials to bring this place to

Thee._____ Be - hold, we come, dear_ Lord,_____ foot - sore and

wea - ry;_____ O bless this house we con - se - crate to Thee.

A - men,__ a - men, be it so._____

Use Me in Your Kingdom

(Commissioning service)

M. L.

Easy folk

Mosie Lister

Take my life,_____ take it now__ and use me, Lord._____

Use me in __ Your king-dom; an-y - where will do._____ A

ser-vant, Lord._____ I want to be a ser-vant, Lord.

Let me be__ Your dis - ci - ple, let me fol - low You._____

If my own strength should ev - er fail,_____ Lord, stay be -

One World, One Lord

(Celebrating the Church, promoting the program)

N. H.

Nancy Harrison

Militantly

1. One world, one Lord,___ one hope for all man-kind; One gold - en cord___ u - nit - ing kin - dred minds. All hon - or and glo - ry to the God who dwells a - bove! One world, one Lord, ___ one fel - low - ship of love.

2. One world, one Lord;___ in Him we are com - plete. In one ac - cord___ we wor - ship at His feet. God's wis - dom has formed us; we are made by His de - sign. One world, one Lord, ___ one fel - low - ship di - vine.

3. To ev - 'ry na - tion goes the gos - pel call; His great sal - va - tion of - fered un - to all. God's mer - cy is end - less; He is guard - ing all our days. One world, one Lord, ___ one fel - low - ship of praise!